keep it simple

nick page

keep it simple

[and get more out of life]

HarperCollins*Publishers*

HarperCollins*Publishers*
77–85 Fulham Palace Road, London W6 8JB

First published in Great Britain in 1999
by HarperCollins*Publishers*

© 1999 Nick Page

1 3 5 7 9 10 8 6 4 2

Nick Page asserts the moral right to be
identified as the author of this work

A catalogue record for this book is
available from the British Library

ISBN 0 00 274023 0

Printed and bound in Great Britain by
Woolnough Bookbinding Ltd, Irthlingborough, Northamptonshire

contents

keep it simple

To affect the quality of the day,
that is the highest of arts.
Henry D. Thoreau

Never mind the job,
some of us want a life.
Newspaper headline

Blissful are the simple, for they
shall have much peace.
Thomas à Kempis

more life, less complications

The aim of this book is simply to help you get more
out of life. In these few pages, I hope to show you
that it is possible to live a life that is less stressful
and more fulfilling: a life that is not lived in thrall
to money, or your job, but which is rich with possibilities.

This book is a journey into what you really want to do and who you really want to be. Along the way we will look together at ways to beat all the things that conspire to clutter up our lives and rob us of time, money and energy. We will be travelling together, because I too am a complexity addict who is trying to kick the habit. I have two small children, a working wife and a mortgage that rivals the national debt of a small South American country. But I believe that it is possible to find a simple way of life that is achievable in modern society. We can all learn to live more simply, even while paying the mortgage and holding down a job.

So if you've ever thought that life could be better; if you've ever wanted more time or less stress; if you've ever wanted things to be more simple; then this book is for you.

the perpetual rush hour

'If I leave the office no later than 5.12 p.m. I can just make the 5.50 p.m. train from London. If that makes it back on time, I will just be in time to catch the 6.47 p.m. bus home, providing I sprint from the station to the bus stop. Any variance in these timings and I could be in for a long wait.'

Sound familiar? For many of us, life is one long struggle to make connections. You run to catch the tube, so you can run to catch the train, so you can run to catch the bus. You rush to complete the shopping, so that you can run to pick up the kids, so that you can leap about making the tea. If all goes well, you might just have the energy to collapse in an exhausted heap in front of the TV. Then it's off to bed before it all starts again...

Secretly we all know that life isn't meant to be this complicated, but we don't know how to slow it down. We're tied into the timetable, afraid to miss a connection. Our lives are a complicated network of meetings, appointments and commitments that we just can't avoid. There is always the fear that the moment we stop running, the whole rickety edifice will come crashing down.

The great news is that life doesn't have to be this way. There are things we can do to change. There are practices we can adopt, ideas we can use, patterns to follow which will allow us to take control of our lives. We can escape the timetable and make our own decisions. Instead of following the tracks that others lay down for us we can step off the treadmill and start to live deliberately.

living deliberately

We live deliberately when:

- we decide to buy what we want, instead of what others say we should want.
- we think for ourselves, instead of being told what to think.
- we recognize that there are some things that are more important than money.
- we fulfil the demands of our work without being controlled by it.
- we find space in our life to think, pray and relax.
- we value and nurture our relationships.
- we live in a way that is self-determined, original and fulfilling.

Above all, we live deliberately, when we develop our own consciously-chosen lifestyle to replace the one we were sold 'off the peg.'

A simple life is a deliberate life. It is not necessarily a life of abstinence, or even self-denial; it is rather a life of control; the life we want, rather than the one we were given.

keep it simple

your journey, your choices

Before we set out on the journey, a word of caution.
Achieving simplicity is not, in itself, simple. It re-
quires deep fundamental change, rather than window-
dressing. And real change happens slowly. It occurs in
fits and starts; it is characterized by sudden advances
and frequent setbacks. Slowly, sometimes even
painfully, we have to unlearn old habits, strip away old
ways of working and adopt new practices.

The shelves of bookshops are heaving with vol-
umes of instant schemes to add pounds to your bank
account or lose them from your waist. The latest mir-
acle cream will remove your wrinkles, diet pills will
make you slimmer than a super-model, *Feng Shui*
promises health and wealth if you shift the furniture
around a bit and buy some fish. Minimalism is the
buzz word – antiseptically sparse homes inhabited by
people who dress in black and shave their heads.
Maybe you should become a Shaker – or at least buy
one of their chairs? Or perhaps you should eat
organic food, wear rope sandals and weave your own
yoghurt.

All this is not dealing with the real issue. Good
though some of these things may be (although I
reserve judgment on the rope sandals) what matters is

attitude, rather than *appearance*. You do not achieve simplicity by altering your dress or having an architect 'minimalize' your house.

So, although this book contains hundreds of ideas to help you simplify your life, it is not a 'get simple quick' book. Some ideas may make a huge difference to your life straight away; many will have a smaller impact; a few may have no relevance to you at all. What matters is that *you* decide which ones to try.

thoughts 'r' you

One of the tragedies of late twentieth-century life in our culture is that we don't think very deeply any more. When was the last time you sat down and just pondered something? Too often our ideas, responses and even our fundamental beliefs come pre-packaged, shrink-wrapped and purchased wholesale at the local branch of 'Thoughts 'R' Us'.

Your mind is too sacred a place to allow others to furnish it for you. If you truly desire to simplify your life, then you will need to swim against the tide, for from all sides we are assailed by those who wish to sell us something, lend us money, recruit us for the cause or simply waste our time.

Simplicity comes from inside. It comes from a willingness to change, to march to the beat of a different drum. It is reflected in our possessions and our lifestyles, but its origin lies in our hearts.

There is a Japanese proverb which says 'The journey is also the destination.' We are all travellers, and we will be travellers all our lives. Let's accept that and move on in the knowledge that the journey is worth making and that life can be better, less stressful, more fulfilling if we can truly learn to Keep It Simple.

a rule of life

as quiet as a monk

What do you think of when you picture a monastery? Most of us think of silence and contemplation, of hooded figures working in peace and quiet; a different world, as silent and serene as a limpid pool.

In fact, monasteries are busy, active places. Monks have jobs to do and tasks to fulfil. The monastic life is one of the most disciplined lives imaginable. And that is the key to their sense of calm. It is not that there are less demands on their time, it is rather that they all know the rules. All monks, of whatever order, follow their particular 'rule of life'. This tells them how to live, what kinds of work they should be doing, how they should behave and how their day is ordered.

I do not want to romanticize the monastic life – it is hard and rigorous. Most of us don't want to enter a monastery. We are not interested in shaving our heads, wearing sandals and learning how to chant. We just want the world to slow down a little.

But I do not need to become a monk to learn from them, to bring a little of their serenity and order into my life. It is possible to take a monastic approach to life without being a monk. All we have to do is create our own 'rule of life'.

a rule of life

The fact is that all of us obey rules – it's just that most of them are unwritten. It is these unwritten rules and assumptions that make our lives so complex:

- I must work until 7 each night.
- I must earn more money next year.
- I must attend those meetings.
- I must get promotion.

These are not *our* rules. We didn't create them. We were presented with them as a *fait accompli*. But it doesn't have to be that way. We can change the rules and replace them with guidelines of our own.

Your rule of life will be a statement of what you want out of your life, and just as importantly, what you *don't* want out of life. Your rule will help you to decide what your priorities are and what kind of work you should do. It will help you to allocate your time, give priority to what is important, and get rid of all the stuff which makes live so cluttered.

how to create a rule

In this book I want to concentrate on five main areas which are crucial to the quality of life: quietness, possessions, work, money and relationships. As you read through the book, start to put together your rule. Make a note of ideas that appeal to you and commit yourself to putting them into action.

For example you may decide to:

- spend one weekend a year just being quiet.
- leave work half an hour earlier.
- get rid of your credit card debts.

What you decide is up to you. But write it down. Then you will have a list of decisions, a list of things that you are going to do, commitments you are going to make, targets at which you are aiming. You will have your rule of life.

simple quietness

All the troubles of life come upon
us because we refuse to sit quietly
for a while each day in our rooms.
Blaise Pascal

Go, sit in your cell, and your cell
will teach you everything.
Abbot Moses of Scete

talk less, think more

We live in a noisy world. Much of the stress people
experience at work and at home is caused by noise.
The phone, the boss, the kids, the endless demands...

In medieval times, if people wanted to torture an
enemy, they would create unrelenting noise, banging
drums and ringing bells day and night until the constant clamour drove the victim insane. In recent times
US troops have used loud speakers blaring constant
rock music to force people out of hiding.

Quietness is the mortar that holds the bricks of our lives together. It fills the spaces and seeps into the cracks. Without it, the whole house starts to shake. Constant noise creates stress, but quietness creates calm.

The first part of our rule, therefore, is quietness. Quietness not only recharges our batteries, it gives us space to think deeply about the other aspects of our lives that need simplifying. We begin with quietness because without 'thinking time' nothing else in our lives will ever be truly simple.

In this section you will find ideas on:

- creating silence at home.
- controlling demands on your time.
- taming the telephone.
- simple relaxation.
- bringing more quietness into your life.

it's good not to talk

'The disciple is to be silent and listen,' runs the rule of Saint Benedict. How rarely we do either! We are so used to speaking, persuading, manipulating, complaining and ordering others about.

In Douglas Adams' *The Hitch Hiker's Guide to the Galaxy*, Ford Prefect wonders why humans are always talking. He forms a theory: if humans don't speak, their mouths probably seize up. Later he revises this theory: if humans don't keep exercising their lips, their *brains* start working.

Try to catch moments of silence. Even in the middle of a busy day it is possible to find five minutes when you don't have to say anything. Go for a walk (without the Walkman). Sit on a bench. Shut your office door. Stop speaking for a moment and let your brain start working.

Silence allows us to explore our own minds. Tragically we know much about the world, but little about ourselves. Few of us really understand ourselves – our hopes, dreams, aspirations and motivations. This is because these things are buried deep inside us and only quietness and solitude give us the tools for excavation.

how to create silence

There are simple ways to create silence. They take some willpower, and maybe some organization. But in lives that feel battered by noise, here are some ways to turn down the volume.

try turning off the tv

It is amazing how that box dominates our lives. We instinctively turn to it the moment we get home, the remote control in our hands, flicking from channel to channel. Research has shown that the average time spent watching any one channel is less than two minutes. The TV has become as fragmented and hectic as our lives.

One of the easiest ways to create some space is to keep the TV turned off for an evening. Spend the time in another way. Read a book. Read *this* book. Go for a walk. Talk to your family. Do anything, but don't just settle in front of the box.

learn to say 'no'

Many of us are 'needs-driven people'. When someone asks us to do something, we cannot resist rushing in. It doesn't matter that we are now fully booked up for the next five years:

- can you house this meeting on Monday night?
- can you join the committee?
- can you help out with the arrangements?

Our hearts begin to pound, our pulses race. Monday was the one night we had free. But this is such a worthy cause! It would be wrong to turn it down.

Face facts: it is no good complaining that your life is too full when you are the one who is cramming every waking moment with commitments. I am not arguing that you should not volunteer for some things, or put yourself out for others. What I am saying is that if all the good deeds you are doing, committees you are attending, meetings you are chairing and the people you are helping are causing you to lie awake at night stressed out, then something is wrong.

Decide which commitments are really important and stick to them. Decide also how many nights of the week you are going to be available for these commitments and do not be tempted to shift things about. You do not have to justify your use of personal time to outsiders. Balance your life. The only person who should be in charge of your time is you.

tame the tyranny of the telephone

There is something tyrannical about the telephone. Every time it rings, no matter what we are doing, we stop and answer it. It doesn't matter if we're in the middle of an important conversation, we just stop in the middle of a sentence and pick the thing up. If a person were to interrupt in this way we would consider them rude.

Phones are massive interrupters of life, but there is a very simple way to limit their power: don't answer them. There's no immutable law of the universe stating that you have to drop everything and answer the phone, or leap out of the bath when it rings. I know of one household, for example, where they don't answer the phone during mealtimes. Mealtimes are for the family, and no-one is allowed to interrupt that.

Some people feel unable to ignore a ringing phone. Try any of the following:

- turn off the sound, or unplug it at the socket. You won't hear it ring.
- switch the answerphone on.
- wait until it is finished and use a 'last caller' system to find out who called. If you don't recognize the number it was probably not very important.

go for a walk
You can find space by just going out for a walk. Don't worry about a destination, just go for a relaxed stroll. We spend too much of our time rushing *to* somewhere – it is sometimes nice to chance upon a different, unexpected destination.

book a meeting with yourself (i)

If your life is dominated by meetings and appointments, you are going to have to use guerrilla tactics. Treat yourself like one of those outside forces who are making demands on you. Book out evenings for meetings with yourself. Mark it in the diary. It is an appointment that must be kept. If you need to get a baby-sitter, fine. We are keen to get a baby-sitter when we need to go out to the cinema or theatre or restaurant – but spending time in quiet is just as important as any of these. Use this time to sit and relax, or think and plan. Keep it quiet.

advance by retreating

> The only excuse for a retreat
> is so you can advance later.
> *Napoleon Bonaparte*

If you want space and quiet, then why not go on a retreat? Just as the ancient monks spent time alone in their cell, you can visit a retreat house to read, to pray, and to think. A retreat is simply some time – normally at least a day – spent on your own. For Christians retreats involve prayer and meditation. Some people go on retreat when they want guidance over a particular issue, others go regularly, using quietness and solitude to recharge their batteries.

Of course you don't have to go to a retreat house: you can go away on your own. The key thing is to spend time on your own, away from the noise and the hurly-burly of your life.

the fast show

One of the best ways to make space in our lives is to deliberately abstain from a particular activity. For example, we might go without food for a day or so, or do without TV for a week; we might choose to forego newspapers, or the golf course, or the weekly trip to the shopping centre.

This is 'fasting'. It is not designed as a kind of masochistic trial of strength – it is rather a shifting of priorities in order to concentrate on something more important.

Going without a meal creates space – and not merely in your stomach. Use the time that you would have spent preparing, buying or eating the food in silence. You might choose to spend the time praying, meditating, reading a book or planning your life. We spend so much time nourishing our bodies, it is good to reverse the priorities and nourish our souls.

visit a church

In medieval times people who were being hunted for a crime could escape into a church or churchyard and find 'sanctuary'. Their pursuers could not take them out by force but had to wait. Today, churches can be sanctuaries for all of us – places to escape to from the pressures of the working day and the demands that are pursuing us like a pack of hounds.

Churches are quiet places (unless it's time for organ practice). And unless you are part of the Outer Hebrides Mountain Rescue Team, the chances are that you work just round the corner from a church of some kind. They are good places to retreat to at lunchtime or after a particularly stressful day, whatever your religious affiliation or beliefs. Pray if it helps. Or just sit in the quiet and spend a few minutes getting yourself together.

regular servicing

Many people, as adherents to a particular faith, will need to decide on their attendance of religious duties. As a Christian, my rule covers my attendance at church services, the pattern of my prayer life and my reading of the Bible. Church services formed, and still form, the fixed points in a monk's day. For some of us they will provide the foundation for our week.

You may decide to attend a service daily, weekly, monthly, or just once a year to check up on how God is doing. Whatever your choice, decide a plan and stick to it.

Similarly, you may want to commit a certain time each day for devotional time. Again, practice differs widely. Some people start each day with a 'quiet time', a time for prayer and reflection, reading the Bible and preparing for the day ahead. If you are of different beliefs you might choose a different way of preparing: some people read a poem, others go for an early morning stroll.

And of course it doesn't have to be the beginning of the day. The important thing is to find the right time and place for you.

simple relaxation

We have seen that quietness gives us time to consider the really important things, to 'excavate our own life.' But there are times when, after a stressful day at work, all we want to do is relax. Here are some tips.

the right music
Put on a CD of calming music. Something gentle and quiet usually does the trick. (It's not the best moment to put on your Thrash Metal compilation tape.)

light a candle
There is something soothing about a room lit by candlelight. Life moves at a different rate – the light is *slower*. The flame flickers and dances and the modern world recedes.

use aromatherapy oils
Certain aromatherapy oils are excellent for relaxing. Oils like lavender, camomile or geranium can be added to baths or put into oil burners to fill the room with a soothing fragrance.

go to bed
It is hard to be relaxed if you are working long hours and staying out late at night partying. An early night will work wonders.

fathers in the desert

In the fourth century AD, the deserts of the middle east were populated by groups of Christian hermits who began to escape from the clamour of the cities and to live in solitude. Some of them lived solitary lives as hermits; others lived in communities, in monasteries hewn from rock and precariously resisting the sandstorms, the blistering heat and the cold nights.

Their aim was not to leave society to rot, but to show it a different way. They were opting out of the hierarchy and the power games of the 'world'. By choosing to live in a remote and inhospitable place, they were turning the world's value system on its head. They were seeking, in the quiet of the desert, to hear from God. They were not abandoning the world, but searching for truth which the world could follow. Despite their desolate surroundings, they attracted many followers and their fame has spread down the centuries.

There are times when we must be quiet, when we must voluntarily enter the desert. While we are in the world the pressure to conform is immense. Adverts shout at us, long hours drain us of energy, stress gnaws away at us. But in the desert – the place of solitude and quiet – we can truly be ourselves. We can listen and we can learn.

simple possessions

Have nothing in your house
that you do not know to be useful
or believe to be beautiful.
William Morris

Theirs is an endless road, a
hopeless maze, who seek for
goods before they seek for God.
Bernard of Clairvaux

The key to economic prosperity is the
organized creation of dissatisfaction.
Charles Kettering of General Motors

Beware of all enterprises
that require new clothes.
Henry D. Thoreau

buy less, live more

The less we buy, the simpler our life will be. We will have fewer things to worry about, fewer outgoing expenses, less to maintain, to protect, to worry about. We will have more money and fewer debts. And whatever we buy, whether, to use Morris's advice, we are buying something useful or beautiful, it will be *our* choice.

The western world would have us believe that what is important is possession and accumulation. This is not true. Our society is littered with individuals and families who, while outwardly comfortable, have sterile, unhappy and superficial lives. It is perfectly possible to live a deeply fulfilled and happy life without having to rush out and buy everything the shops have to sell you.

In this section you will find ideas on:

- how to buy less.
- buying intelligently.
- getting rid of clutter.
- purging your wardrobe.
- simplifying the kitchen.
- the four Rs – reduce, reject, recycle, and repair.

'i shop, therefore i am'

Shopping has become a way of life. We have ceased to be citizens, inhabitants or even people. Instead we are consumers, dehumanized statistics, defined merely by our ability to purchase things; little more than wallets on legs.

Every weekend the high streets are filled with people who are just shopping. Many of them do not know what they are shopping for. They are not looking for specific goods, they are looking for something less tangible, more fleeting. They are shopping for happiness, for satisfaction, for the transient joy that comes of having 'been to the sales'. And of course, all these things cannot be bought. Adverts tend to link products with emotions: happiness, love, sexual attraction, friendship. 'If you buy my product,' they are saying, 'you will attract beautiful women. You will be elegant, glamorous and sophisticated.' Of course, it doesn't matter that the advert is for toilet disinfectant, we still fall for it.

You are not buying happiness. You are buying a car, a deodorant, a washing powder. Freedom, love and happiness cannot be bought. They can only be given. Don't be fooled.

Simple living means buying what you need, rather

than what the advertisers want you to have. Of course, there are times when it is nice to impulse-buy and I am not necessarily advocating austerity unless this is what you want. But the truth is that much of the time our possessions do not make life better, simpler or even more fun. They just get in the way.

a parable

A friend of mine was in a bicycle shop where he heard a salesman talking to a flashily-dressed young man who wanted to buy a bike.

'It's for the weekend,' said the young man. 'I'm going mountain biking with some guys from work.'

The salesman took the young man round the shop and showed him the options. In the end, the customer settled on the most expensive bike in the shop – a carbon-fibre-framed, shock-absorber-laden super-model of a bike, the envy of every serious mountain-biker, and rolling in at around £2,000.

After the customer had selected his bike, and flashed his Gold Card, he asked about a lock for it.

'Lock?' enquired the salesman. 'What do you want that for?'

'So I can secure it when I leave it somewhere.'

'Let's get one thing straight,' said the salesman sternly, 'you *never* leave this bike unattended. It doesn't matter what lock you put on it, the moment you leave it alone, it will be stolen.'

£2,000 is a lot to pay for a ball and chain. Even one made of carbon fibre.

the four rs

To help us think about our possessions, it is helpful to bear in mind the four Rs: reduce, reject, recycle and repair.

reduce

The basic message is this: buy less. Buying less means less packaging, less expense, less clutter and less to worry about. This is the most fundamental rule of creating a simple lifestyle – reducing our need (some would say our craving) to buy things.

reject

Get rid of everything you don't need, including all that stuff in the attic that 'might come in handy one day' (it never does). We have too many possessions that are neither beautiful nor useful. Reject them.

recycle

We must recycle as much as possible, and this includes not only tins, newspaper and glass, but cardboard, organic matter and clothes. Look for recycled products or products from environmentally sustainable sources.

repair

Most products sold in the west have built-in obsolescence. They are not made to last, as the manufacturers plan to sell you a new one. How often have you heard the phrase 'it's not worth repairing'? If it can be repaired and restored *do it*. Reject planned obsolescence and rescue items from the scrap heap.

how to buy less stuff

So how do we cut down on over-consumption? How do we reduce our spending?

don't go shopping

The simplest way is to avoid temptation completely and not to go into shops. I am not advocating avoiding them completely, it's just that the less you go into shops, the less likely you are to spend money.

know what you want
Be as definite as possible with your shopping. Draw up a list and stick to it. If you are going out to buy a shirt, buy a shirt, not a pair of trousers, three pairs of boots and a new hat.

don't reclassify
When it comes to buying things, we spend a lot of time lying to ourselves:

- I need a new computer.
- I need a new dress.
- I really need a 4-wheel-drive jeep.

There is actually very little in life that we *need*. But there is an awful lot that we *want*. If we reclassify a 'want' as a 'need' we can get it immediately and we don't feel so guilty about rushing out and slapping down the credit card. When standing in the shop with that new pair of shoes, to go with the forty-seven pairs you already have, try saying, 'I want these', instead of 'I need these'. Would you still buy?

the thirty day rule
If you find something that you want, but don't need, leave it before buying. Wait thirty days. If you still

want it then, fine. But often you will find that life has gone on pretty well without it, or that you were just acting on impulse, or that you have found a way round the problem.

build it yourself

When was the last time you built something? I don't mean flat-packed furniture, I mean from scratch? Have you ever made your children a toy? Built them a den to play in? Do you buy your greetings cards or have you ever made them?

Recently I needed new bookshelves. Instead of buying them I built them out of large sheets of MDF. It took me a while, I learnt some new skills and it saved me about £75.

buy nothing day

In Canada an organization called 'Adbusters' sponsors a regular 'buy nothing day', when people are encouraged to spend absolutely nothing at all for an entire day (interestingly enough they have had problems persuading the media to carry adverts for the event). Why not join in? Or even declare your own, more frequent days? You could have 'buy nothing days' once a month or even once a week.

hire it

Don't rush to buy a tool or appliance – you may be able to hire it. My village DIY shop hires out all manner of things, from floor cleaners to drill bits. Obviously if you are going to get a lot of use out of an item, you need to do your sums, but for one-off jobs, hiring is more economical.

how to buy intelligently

The second aspect of simple shopping is to buy more intelligently. This means that we understand what we are buying, choose well and get good value for money.

reject the 4x4 drive effect

The biggest concentration of four-wheel-drive vehicles in the UK is in London. For those of you who might be unfamiliar with London, it is not renowned for its mountainous terrain. Arctic conditions around Piccadilly Circus are rare. The Thames does not burst its banks every monsoon season, roads are not dirt tracks and Oxford Street is hardly ever buried under mud slides, much as we'd like it to be.

So why do you need a four-wheel-drive car in the city? It can't be for the sake of economy as these are big, thirsty, machines. It can't be for the sake of speed, because London is more or less gridlocked anyway, so all vehicles travel at the same speed (except bikes). It can't be because of the heavy loads – as far as I can see, the main use of these vehicles is to take the kids to school, which, unless your children are the size of heifers, you could easily achieve in something smaller than a tank.

No, it can only be the '4x4 effect' – that strange power that causes us to buy something ludicrously overpowered for our use, because it looks good, and everybody else has one.

Creating a simple lifestyle means rejecting the 4x4 effect and buying to fit your requirements, not the requirements of the advertising men.

do you need the latest model?
In the world of computers, the word of the moment is always 'upgrade'. A program is released, and a few months later a new, even better version arrives, bursting with features we didn't even know we wanted. Like little cyber-lemmings we rush out and upgrade immediately. After all – you have to run the latest version, don't you? Just as you have to dress in the latest fashions, and drive a new car bristling with new features. It's not that we actually need those new

features – it's just that we are desperate to have the 'latest thing'.

You do not necessarily need the latest model. Try buying an older or second-hand version. The latest upgrade might offer you features which will make life a lot better. It might open up a whole new range of possibilities. Or it might simply empty your wallet faster than a hyperactive pickpocket. Think before you buy.

not cost, but value
Often choosing the cheapest item is counter-productive. Instead choose with care – try to find items that will last. A well-made pair of shoes will probably not be cheap. But they will last for many years after that 'bargain' pair have fallen to pieces.

It's not a question of cost, but of value. Fresh food might cost more than a cheap take-away, but its value is greater since it is better for you. Similarly, higher quality tools, although more expensive, offer better value for money, since they last longer. Think about what you buy and use your money wisely. It will be simpler in the long run.

understand the hidden cost

Everything we buy comes at a price – and not just the price on the label. Most of the time we don't recognize this hidden cost. We are so besotted with the object itself, we don't notice the add-ons, the extras and the additional expense in time, energy and money.

For example, how many times have you bought an item of clothing only to find out it was 'Dry Clean Only' – meaning extra time and expense? Have you ever considered what your electricity bill would be like if you didn't have the dishwasher, washing machine, deep-fat fryer, computer, air-conditioner and lava lamp? What would your phone bill be like if you didn't have that modem? How much would you have saved over the years had you used a car with a smaller engine? And did you know how expensive the refill cartridges were going to be for that smart new laser-printer?

I am not necessarily saying that we should do without these things (personally, I think the invention of the dishwasher ranks up there with penicillin), only that they all cost us a lot more than merely what we pay to get them. Check the hidden extras – they may be more than you are prepared to pay.

how to own less

A few months ago I moved house. As our possessions slowly and inexorably filled the huge lorry, I was shocked at the amount I had managed to accumulate. So many purchases which seemed a good idea at the time, so many books I meant to read but never got round to, games I would never play again, clothes I could no longer get into, kitchen gadgets I'd never used ... well, you get the idea.The truth is that we don't need half of the stuff that fills our houses. Here are some ways to get rid of clutter and slow down the accumulation.

be ruthless
Look around you at all you have in your house. How much do you regularly use? Be ruthless. If that fondue set has been sitting at the back of the cupboard for seven years it's a fair bet you'll never use it. Bin it, sell it, or adapt it to some other purpose.

boot out the clutter
Several times a year my wife and I collect together a load of stuff and go to a car boot sale. It's a great chance to convert all that useless clutter into useful money.

the simple kitchen

'From behind my ovens,' wrote the great chef Carême, 'I feel the ugly edifice of routine crumbling beneath my hands.' I must admit I share his feelings – if not his culinary skill. There are few things I enjoy more than pottering about in the kitchen making something to eat. Yet for many of us, in our hurly-burly lives, the kitchen is the place where the microwave is used to reheat instant meals. There is nothing wrong with ready-to-eat meals, but a constant diet of quick snacks and boil-in-the-bags is unhealthy and expensive. Here are some ideas to bring simplicity into the kitchen.

learn to improvise
Mastering some basic cookery techniques will mean that you can improvise meals – making the most of the food you have in the house, without having to rush out to the take-away again.

use all your stores
Every so often, instead of shopping, use what you've got – but check that it hasn't gone past its sell-by date first! Much of the time we assume that 'we haven't got a thing to eat', when with a bit of invention there is

enough for a perfectly decent meal. Empty those cupboards before adding new stuff.

quality counts (i)
Good, fresh food takes longer to cook than stuff out of tins, but is worth the (minimal) effort.

quality counts (ii)
Buy good quality equipment if you can afford it. Good saucepans will last you 25 years.

get the most out of your meals
A roast chicken one day can provide a cold chicken salad the next, and some chicken broth. A pot roast will provide the base for further stews and soups. Leftovers can be great (anyone for bubble and squeak?).

pick your own
Not all of us are up to growing our own produce, but there's no doubt it's great to eat stuff from your own garden. At the very least, try to grow some fresh herbs. You can also pick blackberries from the hedgerows and – if you're ultra-keen – mushrooms from the fields (make sure you identify your mushrooms correctly).

the simple wardrobe

purge your wardrobe

Most of us have too many clothes. Our wardrobes are full of items that we don't wear, can no longer get into, or wouldn't be seen dead in.

Simplify your wardrobe. Go through it and ask yourself when you last wore each item. If the answer is 'over 6 months ago' consider whether or not you really need it. If the answer is 'over a year ago', you definitely don't need it. Give the clothes away to a charity shop or take them to a car boot sale. Purging your wardrobe means less washing, less worry and a simpler life.

buy one, chuck one

When you buy something try to get rid of something else (die-hard simplifiers advocate getting rid of two items for every one you buy). Whenever I buy new clothes I have a look through to see if there is anything I want to get rid of in my wardrobe. There is usually something that is worn out, unused or, sadly, doesn't fit any more.

resist the lure of the label

> Fashion is made to become unfashionable.
> *Coco Chanel*

How often have you been tempted to buy something because of the label?

'Alright, it cost twice as much as the other suit and I have to take shallower breaths just to fit in the thing, but it's an *Armani* for heaven's sake!'

Think before you buy:

- is this good value?
- will I wear it a lot?
- is it well made?
- will it last?
- do I really need it?

Freeing yourself from the lure of the labels means that you will never have to worry whether you are fashionable or not. If you like it and it offers good value then buy it. If not, don't.

find your own style
Choose clothes that you feel comfortable in, and styles that will last. Chasing fashion only means that in a

year those bell-bottom leopard-print loon-pants that looked so cool in the shop will look ludicrous. But your own style will last. The colours that suit you, the clothes you genuinely like (rather than *think* you ought to like), are good investments.

avoid ironing

In Greek mythology one of the characters in Hades was called Sisyphus. His punishment was to roll a stone up a hill to the top and, just when he thought he had made it, it would roll down again. Nowadays he would just be given the ironing to do. Ironing is the bane of many lives. No matter what we do, that pile in the corner never seems to go down. It is always there, lurking.

There are some ways in which you can reduce it. First, don't iron anything that doesn't need it. I don't care what anyone says, underwear does not need to be ironed. Nor do towels, hankies, socks, etc. (Some friends of ours only ever iron the bits that are visible e.g. the front of shirts. They argue that, since they are going to wear either pullovers or jackets, no-one will see the back. And if it's too hot and you want to take your jacket off your shirt will be crumpled anyway.)

Second, choose clothes made in crease-resistant fabrics which do not need ironing. These strike me as one of the great inventions of modern life.

Third, dry your clothes in the fresh air (or using a dryer if you must) and hang them out straight away. A lot of the creases will drop out.

Finally, the most drastic measure, give up. Try looking crumpled, but interesting.

simple recycling

Simple living should look beyond self-interest. We have a duty to recycle all we can. Within our houses that means reusing packaging to store other things, putting organic matter onto a compost heap or saving old wood to provide heat or building materials. Be inventive. Tins and bottles can be recycled, old clothes can be put in a 'clothes bank' and even old shoes can be recycled. Your council will probably have information on its policies and resources available.

simple repairing

If you're like me, you will often have bought something new, rather than getting the old one repaired. Or you will have been told by an expert – 'you'll be better off buying a new one, mate.'

We should, instead, seek to repair all we can. This may mean gaining skills which we don't presently have. I am aware I have a lot to learn about plumbing, electricity and cars. But I also know that unique feeling of satisfaction when I have repaired something that was broken. It's not only about saving money, it's about consuming less. Be a repairer, not a serial consumer.

life in the woods

In the long run men hit only what they aim at. Therefore, though they fail immediately, they had better aim at something high.

Henry D. Thoreau

On 4 July 1845, Henry David Thoreau started an experiment – to live in the woods on the minimum needed to keep him alive. The record of his life – *Walden, or Life in the Woods* – is one of the classic texts of simple living. His aim was to live a truly independent life, working the minimum needed to survive. Living with the utmost simplicity, he discovered that by working for about six weeks each year he could meet all his expenses.

Thoreau wanted to be free. He took delight in the world around him and he rejected the idea of perpetually accumulating money and possessions. He challenged the status quo. He was jailed for his refusal to pay a poll tax to a government involved in what he saw as an unjust war. He was opposed to slavery, and actively helped fugitive slaves escape.

'The mass of men lead lives of quiet desperation,' he wrote. Today, it is not hard to see that same desperation etched into the faces of the people crammed into the trains and buses. Not many of us are likely to end up building our own house and living by a pond (not to mention eating roast rat). But Thoreau has much to teach us about what is truly necessary to live a deep and meaningful life.

simple work

No amount of pay ever made a good
soldier, a good teacher, a good artist
or a good workman.

John Ruskin

One must not always think so much
about what one should do, but rather what
one must be. Our works do not ennoble us,
but we must ennoble our works.

Meister Eckhart

I like work, it fascinates me.
I can sit and look at it for hours.

Jerome K. Jerome

work less, achieve more

When someone loves their work, it is reflected in their
life. When you enjoy what you do, and find it fulfilling, interesting and worthwhile, then everything

changes. What a shame, therefore, that for so many people today, work is a mixture of stress, tiredness, exasperation and worry.

In this section you will find ideas on:

- finding out if you are in the 'right livelihood'.
- working shorter hours.
- working more effectively.
- dealing with distractions.
- finding more time.
- beating the computer!

First though, we have to look at some more fundamental questions. Are you in the right job? Do you really need to work so hard?

you can't have your cake and eat it

There are a lot of people making pots of money selling you quick-fix solutions that will allow you to keep your high-profile, highly-paid job, whilst at the same time enjoying a full social life, taking several University degrees, raising four children and learning to scuba dive.

Here's the truth: it can't be done.

If you want to simplify your life, great. But let's not kid ourselves. You can't have it all. You will have to make choices along the way, and our relationship with work is where we see those choices in their starkest form. Ultimately, if you are caught in a job that causes you stress, keeps you from what's important and only adds complexity to your life, the only solution is to change jobs.

Many people have opted for a job which pays less, but which carries a lighter burden. Others – like myself – have chosen to go freelance, accepting that the pleasure of managing your own time is balanced by the risk of not getting enough work. There are ways to reduce stress in your workplace, manage your time better and cut down on the hours you work – and in this section I hope to share some of those with you. But it may be that you need to make hard choices and tough decisions.

right livelihood

The first consideration when it comes to simplifying your work is to make sure you are in the right job to start with. You might find it useful to use the Buddhist concept of 'right livelihood'. This means examining what you do for a living and asking four simple questions about it:

- will I be able to do this job for a long time?
- does this job benefit the community?
- do I enjoy what I am doing?
- is my work giving me a sense of fulfilment?

If the answer is 'no' to all four, you are probably in the wrong job – your livelihood is wrong. That doesn't necessarily mean you should just throw it over immediately, but it does mean that, long-term, this job is taking you nowhere.

Your life will never be simple if you are in the wrong job, no matter how well you manage your time or how productive you are. Find out what you do best, and, as best you can, do it.

how many hours?

People in Britain today work the longest hours in Europe. The reasons are many and various: some fear losing their job; others want to make more money; some people get their sense of fulfilment and self-worth from their job; in some, sad cases, people work long hours simply to avoid going home. Whatever the reason, and wherever we live and work, we have to face the truth that what we do is not who we *are*. Sooner or later, we are all going to be on our own.

What is the point of holding down that sixty-hour a week, high profile job, if your private and personal life is falling apart? As part of your rule you must decide the hours you are going to work and stick to them.

This is not easy. Many jobs these days make demands on us that are at best inconvenient, and at worst damaging to our health. The time has come to fight back a little.

cutting down

There is only one way to cut down long hours: go home earlier. But if you are in a job where you have been accustomed to work until 7.00 p.m., suddenly leaving on the dot of 5.00 p.m. is an impossible leap.

small doses

One trick is to shave the minutes off gradually. Start by leaving a quarter of an hour earlier. Make sure you stick to the routine for a week. The chances are that it will not have made a huge difference to your work.

The following week shave another fifteen minutes off – and keep doing this until you reach a time you are contented with and which fulfils the demands of the job.

safe days

Another option is to limit your overtime to certain days and to commit yourself to leaving on time on others. Most people already do this, especially on Fridays. You might decide that Mondays and Wednesdays are your late days. Leave on time for the rest of the week. The important thing is to create a timetable and stick to it. Of course there will always be emergencies, but ultimately no one is going to come up to you and suggest you leave on time. It is your job to do it for yourself.

simple work

The next thing is to look at our work practices and to try to identify where the stresses occur. Naturally this will be different with each job. The trick is to find the practices that help *you* and to integrate them into your work. Too many time-management systems try to make you conform to a way of working that is alien and unhelpful. A better way is to find out how best you work and try to maximize that.

Nevertheless, there are certain things that we can all do to make our work lives simpler.

log your time

Few of us know where all the hours that we spend at work really go. The day whizzes by, we hardly seem to get a thing done, but we don't know where exactly the time has gone.

The first thing to do is to log your time. Draw up a sheet of paper that divides the day into 15-minute sections. For each of these sections record what you were actually doing. Were you on the phone, dealing with interruptions, talking to clients, making coffee, or redrafting that report for the seventieth time? Once you see where your time goes you will be able to identify which bits are sheer wastage and start to take action.

do one thing at a time

In the world of computers, the big buzz word is 'multi-tasking', the ability of a computer to do more than one thing at once. Humans do this naturally – we can be doing the ironing, thinking about work and listening to the radio at the same time. The trouble is, we do it *too* naturally. We try to do too many things at once.

Do one thing at a time, and do it well. While you are doing it, focus your attention on that task alone, and try not to let other things distract or concern you. At work, try to restrict yourself to one task at a time and complete it as near as you can. A lot of half-finished tasks are a sure cause of stress and anxiety.

organize your environment
We feel less stressed if there is less clutter around us. Your desk doesn't have to be clear, but it should be organized. There should be a reason – however frivolous – for things being there.

keep it brief
Never mind cleanliness, brevity is next to godliness if you ask me. We over-produce. Reports take eight pages where they could take one. Meetings last all morning when they could have been dealt with in half an hour.

Make sure that all meetings have a clear agenda and try to stick to it. Arrive on time, and where possible leave at the time specified.

Try to keep your reports as short as possible. It is said that when John Harvey Jones became head of ICI he issued an edict that all reports should be no longer than one side of A4. This caused enormous problems for his managers who were used to issuing reports that ran on for pages and pages. The truth is that most reports try to say too much. Keep it brief – and ask others to do the same.

work at home
If it is possible do some work at home. Increasingly, businesses are recognizing the benefits of allowing staff to work at home. It is a more relaxed and frequently more productive environment.

organize your tasks
Making lists generally helps. I am not a great list-maker, but I do find it a good way of relieving stress. When I am anxious, or trying to juggle many different projects, making a list of what needs doing when calms me down.

book a meeting with yourself (ii)
Treat yourself as a client. Book a work meeting with yourself. Put it in your diary as a priority item. Then you will always be sure of time to do what you need to do, free from meetings and interruptions. If you need to, book a half day or a day each week without meetings of any sort. You will find that you have the time to consider the important things and to pick up on all those loose ends.

Now go through your diary and book these meetings for the next six months. This time is just as important – and will probably be a great deal more productive – than all the meetings that would otherwise fill the day.

simple computing

'We shape our tools,' wrote Marshall McLuhan, 'and then our tools shape us.' Few tools demonstrate this as clearly as the computer – a machine that was designed to create the 'paperless office' and has since succeeded in spewing out more paper than ever before. Nevertheless, the computer can be a valuable tool in our quest for simplicity – as long as *we* master *it* and *it* does not master *us*.

read the manual
Most people who use a computer don't understand their machine. It is an alien being to them, an unruly animal that has to be persuaded, cajoled or occasionally beaten into submission, but which more often beats us.

Ignorance is not bliss when it comes to computing. Try to get to know your machine. Go on courses;

read the manual, or a book about the software. Understand the basics of how it works.

master the program

Eighty per cent of computer users use only 20 per cent of the program's capabilities. Most people I know use their computer as a kind of glorified electronic typewriter. The most common remark I get when explaining computer programs to people is, 'I didn't know it could do that!' Again, training is the answer. Get your company to send you on a course, or work through a simple book. Don't just stop when it does what you think it ought to do: go beyond that. See what more the program can offer you.

use macros and glossaries

Macros are small programs within software that automate repetitive tasks. They can be used to input frequently-used text (such as addresses, signatures, etc.), save regularly, open other programs, cut and paste and many other tasks which you perform frequently.

Glossaries are programs that replace codes for frequently-used words or phrases. For example, my glossary program allows me to type 'cd' and automatically expands it to 'could'.

filter that e-mail

E-mail is a great invention. I use it all the time. However, the problem with e-mail is that it's just *too* easy. Many people in office situations receive hundreds of e-mails each day. Most of these aren't worth reading and have only been sent because the person sending them wants to cover their back, or wants to say something but is too idle/injured/tied to their computer to get up from their chair and walk across the room. Unfortunately there is no easy solution to this, but one way is to use a filtering system. Any e-mail program worth its salt will have a feature where you can automatically assign certain e-mails to certain folders. Other than that, the only real way of stopping e-mail overload is to create a culture where people are encouraged to talk to each other rather than bombard their colleagues with electronic text.

only use it when you need it

Because computers are so powerful we think we have to use them for everything. But sometimes the old-fashioned way is best. For example, a hand-written letter or memo is quicker to produce than a computer-typed one. If what you have to say is simple, uncontroversial and does not have to be reproduced twenty times with full columns and italics, then just write it yourself (that pointy thing is called a pen).

Similarly, your memos do not have to be a work of art. Laying them out in Florentine swash capitals with full-colour illustrations does not necessarily make them any more readable. By all means make them well-designed and creative, but remember that it's just a memo – not the roof of the Sistine Chapel.

simple money

If you make money your God,
it will plague you like the devil.
Henry Fielding

Money has never yet made anyone rich.
Seneca

Make all you can, save all you can,
give all you can.
John Wesley

The love of money is the
root of all evil.
Paul of Tarsus

earn less, gain more

Most of us labour under the delusion that life would be
less complicated if we were rich. Seriously rich. Lottery-
sized rich. Each week in our millions, we fill in the

ticket and hope for the finger to descend and a heavenly voice to say, 'It could be you.'

But it can be you already. If you can control your money then your life will be simpler. You will have less stress, fewer debts, and a richer life. Money is not meant to be our master, but our servant. This may seem like an impossible dream, but there are many thousands of people who have learnt that it is possible to live a 'rich' life with less money. They might earn less, but they are doing what they want to do and living deliberately.

In this section you will find ideas on:

* finding out what you really earn.
* living within your means.
* effective budgeting.
* getting out of credit card debt.
* saving money in the home.
* spending less in the shops.

all aboard the gravy train

I was sitting on a train a few years back and got talking to the man next to me. We chatted about what I did and what he did. At Oxford, he gave me a lift home in his car and just as he dropped me off, he turned to me and said, 'You know, Nick, I wonder what it's all about sometimes. I work fourteen-hour days to make all the money I can and it doesn't seem to mean anything at all.' I have never seen that man since. I pray he's found some answers to the questions that seemed to be plaguing him. But his life illustrates only too well the lie we have been sold: that more money equals a better life.

For example, a recent survey revealed that whilst 80 per cent of British adults felt they had all the material comfort that they needed, only one in five felt fulfilled by their lives. Money cannot make you happy. The best it can promise is that you will be unhappy in comfort.

I am not romanticizing the joys of poverty, far from it. I have been poor and I have been, if not rich, then well-off. And I prefer well-off. But I can honestly say that I am not any happier than when I was earning a lot less, because my happiness is not contained in a pay packet.

why am i always broke?

We are never really better off, because no matter how much money we get, we always manage to spend it. Expectations rise to match incomes. Indeed, the economist Edward Luttwak has claimed that in America only the top 2 per cent of households has actually benefited from twenty-five years of economic growth. For the rest, the rise in earnings has been matched by the rise in bills.

more life, less money

Keeping it simple means getting more life from less money, and avoiding debt and the stress that comes from over-spending. It means refusing to be tricked into the credit card trap. Above all, it means knowing what you need to live on and living within that.

It is quite possible to live simply on less money. You would not be able to buy that Gucci handbag, it is true, but you would be able to work shorter hours, see more of your family and take life at a gentler pace.

simple budgets

If we are going to simplify our finances we need to know some figures. Knowledge is power – and never more so than where money is concerned.

We need to know how much we actually earn and how much we really need to get by. That information alone will allow us to budget and keep things simple by living within our means.

how much do you earn?

I mean *really* earn. The mistake most of us make is to take the figure that is on our payslip and divide it by the amount of hours on the contract. But that is not actually what you make. Because going to work has all kinds of hidden costs – the amounts you shell out to allow you to appear clean and spotless at your desk on Monday morning.

First, take the overall figure – your salary, then take away your tax and national insurance. Then take away any costs relating to your work – travel, clothing, child care, etc. This is your *real wage* – what you actually earn each year.

how much do you need?

Now go through your bank statements, cheque books, etc. and list all the other payments you must make: the bills for running your home, feeding your family, heating the house, etc. Make sure that you are thorough, but discard anything that is not a necessity of life (that new set of golf clubs, though undoubtedly important, is not that vital). These are your *real costs*.

how much can you spend?

Now take your *real costs* away from your *real wage* and see what the difference is. The likely scenario is that for most of us, what we really *need* to earn is not that huge. It's everything else – what we *want* – that makes up the gap. There is nothing wrong with this, were it not for the fact that most of us budget for the wrong figure. We live according to our fantasy earnings rather than our real wage.

Now you have the information you need to budget correctly. You know how much you actually earn. You know how much you need each month to survive. It's now up to you how you spend the difference.

You may find that this knowledge opens up new opportunities. It is surprising what it costs us to work. Changing your job to one that pays a lot less, but allows you to wear your own clothes, do less commuting and spend less on child care may actually increase your quality of life. Or you may want to work towards investing a larger proportion of your money for the future.

'The truth shall set you free,' says the Bible – and it's true of our personal finances as well. Getting to grips with your finances is one of the greatest steps towards liberty and simplicity.

the black hole

You may find that your real costs are more than your real income. In which case the harsh truth is that you are living above your means. You do not earn enough to cover your outgoings. You will have to either change your job, take on extra work, or cut your expenses. The key thing is not to panic. Take expert advice. Most banks have assistants who will help you look at your finances, or you may like to use an independent advisor. There are also many voluntary agencies that help people with debt problems.

At least now you know the problem. After all, it is only when you know you are in a hole that you can start to build a ladder.

the credit card trap

Another factor is how much you owe. You will probably have included your mortgage, or loan repayments in your fixed outgoings. But what about the other debts? What about credit cards, for instance? For years the card businesses have sold us a lie: they have tried to tell us that when we use the card we are not actually borrowing any money. But of course you are – and at very high rates. Keeping a balance on your card actually costs you a lot of money.

Paying off your credit card bills is one of the single most important things you can do in terms of simplifying your personal finance.

cut them up

Credit cards can, of course, be useful. They are handy for paying big amounts. And certain firms, like car hire companies, won't hire you a car without a credit card. But how many cards do you actually need?

Go through your cards and select one to keep (you might like to keep a store card as well – but be aware that store cards often have even higher rates of interest). Make sure the card you keep does not have an annual fee. Then cut the rest up. You don't need them any more, they lure you into spending what you cannot afford. Get rid of them.

pay them off

If you have balances on the cards, you will need to pay them off. If you cannot afford to pay them off at once – and most of us can't – then you will need to set up a repayment schedule. Set a monthly amount – as far above the minimum amount as you can – to do this. (Do it by direct debit if that helps. Then you know the payments will be on time.)

If you have balances on a number of cards it may not be feasible for you to pay them all off very quickly. The trick is to pay the smallest off first. Keep the others going by paying the minimum payment, but pay as much as you can afford towards the smallest balance. Soon that will be paid off. Then add the amount you were paying for the smallest card to the next highest. Once that is paid off, switch the total amount to the next highest and so on. The rate that you pay off your bills will become faster and faster.

simple shopping

By now you should know how much you have each month to live on. It will be up to you to decide how to spend your money. As we have already seen, simple living means reducing the amount we buy anyway.

But even when we do spend, there are ways to spend less.

keep a spending log
For one month write down everything you spend. At the end of the month you will be able to see exactly how much those triple espressos cost you each morning, how much you are spending on all those little items you take for granted. If some items on your list are non-essential, consider ways to cut them down or do without them completely.

only carry cash
One way to ensure you don't spend more than you can afford is to only carry cash when you go shopping. If you carry no other means of paying – no chequebook, credit or debit cards – you will be unable to exceed your budgeted amount. If, like me, you have hardly any self-discipline to speak of, this is a foolproof method.

bulk buy
Buying items in bulk can give you significant savings. For example, I buy coffee, olive oil and other foodstuffs in bulk from a wholefood co-operative. A 3 litre can of olive oil costs me £11.00. The same brand of

olive oil in 750 cl bottles costs around £5.00–£7.00 in the shops.

Obviously you need to make sure that you can store whatever you buy. Don't buy fresh foods in bulk if you don't have a freezer.

be prepared

Know what you are looking for and don't get drawn into buying something you never intended to. If you really want to maximize your shopping, draw up a shopping list – and stick to it.

step off the pathway

Over the years there has been a lot of research conducted on the way in which we shop. We have been studied like laboratory rats, our responses analysed and tested. You might feel, for example, that you choose where to go in a shop. The truth is, you follow predetermined pathways, in many cases marked out for you. So step off the beaten track. Go and hunt for the bargains that are in the racks at the back.

don't feel obliged to buy

Have you ever wondered why shops display cloths folded up in lovely neat piles, instead of hanging on racks? The truth is, it's got nothing to do with a beautiful display. Studies have shown that customers are more likely to buy clothes that they have unfolded. They've messed up the pile so rather than put the thing back, they take it to the checkout.

Don't feel any obligation to buy. Just dump them in a pile. Someone will refold it. That's what they pay shop assistants for.

check the special offers
Check for fresh goods such as meat which are on special offer as they are close to their sell-by date. Most of this stuff can be frozen. Snap it up, take it home and stick it in the freezer.

Many supermarkets operate multi-buy offers and 3 for the price of 2 offers. As long as it's stuff you want and need and will use, these are worth stocking up on.

ditch the packaging
You will always pay more for pre-packaged food. Buy your cheese at the delicatessen counter and pack your vegetables yourself. You pay up to 50 per cent more for pre-packed, pre-washed, bite-sized potatoes – and anyway, real food has dirt on it.

shop around

Check the prices and specifications before you buy and find out where the cheapest prices are. You can save a lot of money by not buying in the first place you visit.

use mail order

You can often get better value for goods by buying mail order; you also get more time to choose and you can easily return the goods if they are not what you want.

use the internet

Internet shopping is great. You can make big savings on things like books, CDs and computer software. I often buy books from the USA via the web. (Just don't lose track of what you're spending on your credit card.)

simple saving

There are many simple ways in which we can save money and live within our budget. A main area of expense is the home. Consider trying out the following ideas:

- insulate your house to make sure heat doesn't escape. Simple measures like putting draft-excluders round doors and lagging pipes often save more than double glazing.
- turning the thermostat down one degree on your heating will knock 10 per cent off your bill.
- have a shower rather than a bath (it uses a sixth of the water).
- turn off lights and use low-wattage or energy saving bulbs.
- most car journeys are for less than five miles. Where possible walk, or ride a bike.
- only use your dishwasher or washing machine when full.

simple giving

Living deliberately means deciding not only how you are going to spend your money, but how you are going to give it away. For many people, their rule of life will include a figure that they are prepared to give away – perhaps as a percentage of their income. In such cases it is a good idea to decide on such an amount and commit to giving regularly. Most charities, for example, rely on long-term, regular giving. This helps the charities plan and enables them to use the money where it is most needed. Importantly, it also helps *you* plan: you will be able to write in your giving to your budget. Also, by covenanting the money or using gift aid, the charities will be able to recover the tax you have paid on the amount and your gift will be worth even more.

another way

Several years ago I quit my job as Director of a national charity and went back to writing. It was not the stress that made me opt out, although the job was stressful. It was not that I could earn more money by writing – in fact in those early years I earned much less. It was that I was simply fed up.

My first child had been born and I wanted to see her grow up. Instead I was commuting four days a week – a journey of two and a half hours each way. I was not doing what I really wanted to do; I was man-aging a department and not writing. So I became a writer for four days a week and a house-husband for the other one. And my quality of life soared. Because I was no longer travelling I found an extra 20 hours a week. I was no longer eating junk food on station forecourts, or grabbing hurried pub lunches between interminable meetings. I watched my first daughter – and then her sister – grow up.

Of course, there have been times when I have been worried about where the next penny was coming from, and trying to combine raising a family and writing books is often a frustrating task. But the point of this is that it didn't take much to change my life. I have not dropped out – indeed, I still do a lot of work with the charity I left. All it took was a slight redirection, a small step into the unknown.

There is more to life than earning a lot of money. It's just that sometimes we don't do our sums right.

simple relationships

For one human being to love another is perhaps the most difficult task that has been entrusted to us, the ultimate task, the work for which all other work is merely preparation.

Rainer Maria Rilke

God evidently does not intend us to be rich or powerful or great, but he does intend us all to be friends.

Ralph Waldo Emerson

A man of many companions may come to ruin, but there is a friend who sticks closer than a brother.

Proverbs 18:24

less 'me', more 'you'

Life is meant to be shared. It is not a solo occupation. We must treat our friends and families seriously – they are too valuable a part of our lives to be relegated to the odd bits of time that we can spare after everything else. So much of our time is devoted to our possessions – houses, clothes, cars, computers. But these things can never offer the affection, solace, and comfort that is the real stuff of life. Only relationships can give us the sense of belonging that we really need. They are worth nurturing and cherishing, because they make us what we truly are.

In this section you will find ideas on:

• communicating with your partner.
• spending time with your children.
• community involvement.
• relationships in the global village.

communication time

Schedule time for the relationships in your life. It is important to communicate, honestly and openly with your husband or wife, for example. That is difficult to do when the kids are screaming above the noise of the national lottery on TV. (Here's an exercise: hug your TV. Did it feel good?)

Some people put aside a night each week when they sit down with each other to synchronize diaries, allocate tasks and deal with issues which need both partners' concentration. However you organize it – whether on a regular night or less formally arranged – it is vital that both partners communicate honestly and openly and feel 'listened to'. But we should not seek merely to create this 'functional' time, necessary though that is. You also need time when the two of you can talk in depth about things that really matter: not diaries and appointments and gas bills, but hopes, dreams and feelings.

friends, not cliques

Friends are simple. Real friendship has no dress-code, no competition. Real friendship is open, ready to share. Cliques, on the other hand are closed shops. They look inward to the members of the clique alone. They are what C. S. Lewis called 'the inner circle'. But the circle is an ever-decreasing one. Cliques rely on conformity. They exclude those who do not match up.

They are unforgiving. Transgress the rules of the clique and you will be cast out. They will protect you to a point, but beyond that...

Cliques like nothing better than intrigue and gossip. Such things only complicate life. Cliques belong to the world of complexity. Friendship belongs to the world of simplicity.

deep conversations

A wintry morning. A bus stop. The bus was (as usual) late. There were, maybe, 30 people at the stop, all in their heavy winter overcoats, buttoned up to keep out the cold. The air was filled with an eerie silence; despite the group of people there, no human voice was heard. Everyone was lost in their own thoughts, their minds as heavily buttoned up as their coats.

If friendship is going to help us overcome the stresses and strains of our lives then we need to speak with depth to one another. We need, in our lives, people with whom we can be totally honest, friends who we are not afraid to open up to. There are too many buttoned-up people in this world, wrapped up in their problems, with no-one to talk to, lonely in a crowd.

Take time to talk to your friends. Engage in deep conversations. Tell them the truth. Ask for their help. The world is full of superficial chatter. It is full of trite chat-shows peddling their sound-bite solutions. Let us unbutton our minds and sit down in the warmth of friendship.

spend time with your children

I was talking to a group of kids in a classroom about what it means to be a Dad.

'My Dad's great really,' said one boy. 'It's just, he's always buying me things.'

'Is that a problem?' I asked.

'Well, I like the presents,' said the boy, 'but I really wish he'd just spend some time with me.'

Time spent with your children should not be low on your priority list. You may say, 'I'm working so hard in order to give them the best things in life.' But what's the point in working all the hours for your children if they never see you? All you will be is the stranger with the chequebook.

Spending time with children allows you to see things through their eyes. It slows you down (especially if you're trying to walk anywhere with a two-year-old.) Sometimes it enables us to share that childlike wonder in our surroundings. As I walk along the road my daughters are always pointing things out to me. A red flower is a cause for much shouting. A cat is as exotic as a panther. They take an immense joy in things we take for granted. This too is a form of simplicity.

simple speech

'Let your "yes" be "yes", and your "no" be "no".' advises Jesus in the Bible. There is a shortage of trust in the world. We don't believe what we hear, see or read anymore. But the truth is that half the time we are at the very least tempted to lie ourselves. From, 'the cheque's in the post' to, 'I can give up cigarettes any time I want'. We may not engage in great deceit, but the little lies slip easily from our lips. Lying is a complex business. Simple speech is honest speech.

community involvement

One of the things we have to rediscover today is what it means to live as part of a community. As communities we can share things – not only possessions and goods, but insights, advice, abilities. We can also have power. No group is better at changing the community than the inhabitants themselves.

We need to take our communities into account when we think about spending our money. If you shop at a major fast food outlet only one quarter of the money you spend stays in the local area. Shopping at smaller, local concerns might be more expensive, but more of the money stays with the community. I try to buy all I can locally. I value the local services and I don't want to lose them.

Naturally this involves some extra effort. It can cost a bit more. It may not be as time efficient as 'one-stop shopping'. But you might get to know people. And by shopping locally, and supporting local businesses, you will be helping those who cannot make it to the out-of-town superstore.

the global village

Living simply does not mean living without concern. Our commitment to a simple lifestyle is not a self-seeking, inward-looking attitude, but an attempt to redress the balance. We are not just a part of our community, but also a part of the world. We have responsibilities to the other inhabitants in the global village. Like it or not, we are in relationship with them. The training shoes that cost you £80 for a bit of plastic and a fancy label were put together by a teenager working for a pittance in a sweat shop. The tea that wakes us up in the morning has been picked by workers working ten-hour days for pitiful wages.

Wherever possible buy fairly traded goods. Look for Fair Trade labels on goods. This means that more of the money we spend on the product will make its way back to the producer. Find out what you can about the origins of the goods you are buying. What is the company's policy on child labour, trade unions and worker's rights? Use your power as a consumer to help others.

Living simply is not the same as living selfishly. We should use the time we create, the money that we have to fight for a fairer world. To use the old phrase, we should live simply so that others can simply live.

simple truths

the possibilities are endless

I did not set out to write a book, but a list of possibilities. It is up to you where you go from here. Now is the time to start to put together your rule, to look back at all the ideas, suggestions and comments and start to weave them together to form the pattern of your life. Of course, you may already be putting some of these ideas into practice. You have probably come up with some new ideas of your own. It doesn't matter how many or how few ideas you adopt: it's just fantastic that you have set out on the journey.

What is important is not that we follow the same road, but that we all start travelling. Whatever you choose to do, be encouraged. Because the truth is that you will create your own path, a unique path, because no one travels the road in quite the same way. This is not a trial of strength, or a programme that you must follow in every detail. This is a chance to create your own rule – your own statement of who you are, what your values are and what you want out of life.

pursuing the dream

In 1982 Gilbert Kaplan prepared to commit professional suicide. A respected merchant banker and financial publisher, Kaplan proposed to conduct Mahler's *Resurrection* Symphony in front of an invited audience of accountants, politicians and delegates from the International Monetary Fund. The problem was that Kaplan had no formal training beyond Grade I piano lessons. If he were to make a laughing stock of himself, this most trusted pillar of the financial community would never be able to hold his head up in public again. But Kaplan was determined. He booked the Lincoln Centre in New York, hired the American Symphony Orchestra (who insisted that no critics should be present) and issued the invitations.

The concert was unique. As the final great chords sounded, bankers, financiers and seasoned money-men wept and sobbed with emotion. Kaplan received a standing ovation. 'I had the feeling,' he said, 'that they were urging me to fulfil my dream, because each of them had a secret ambition he had not attained. If I had failed, they would have failed too.'

Since then Gilbert Kaplan has become one of the foremost experts on Mahler and has conducted the symphony around the world. I wonder whether all those in his audience have achieved their ambitions and dreams? Or have they buried them deep in the ground, in the hopes that one day they will fade away?

Some Native Americans believe that if a corpse is not buried properly its ghost will come back to haunt you. That's the trouble with untried dreams: they have never been buried and they hang around like ghosts.

the journey is also the destination

In any journey the really important moment is the first step. So often we don't make it beyond the planning. We study maps, look at pictures, read books, but we never take that first step.

Don't worry that you will stumble. We all do. The road is not straightforward and there are rough paths along the way. We are all learners and we will always be learners. Don't worry that you will fail sometimes, worry only that you will persevere.The world is full of 'might-have' people; those who always meant to do something, but who somehow kept putting it off. Many of us dream of living a simpler life. Many of us dream of having more time, less anxiety, less pressures.

It's time to stop dreaming and start living. It's time to Keep It Simple.